AWAKENING THE TRUE SELF

Awakening the True Self

Alan Jones' Spiritual Odyssey

BRIANNA LAFFERTY

Alan Jones

BriOnic LLC

Contents

SPIRITUAL AWAKENING: THE TURNING POINT

Preface

This book tells the story of Alan's journey to his authentic, spiritual self, a journey marked by profound experiences, deep introspection, and transformative realizations. I am honored to write Alan's story, not just because of the extraordinary synchronicities that brought us together, but also because of the meaningful purpose it serves in his life and beyond.

Our paths first crossed when Alan saw me on the event flyer as a speaker for the Near-Death Experience (NDE) group in Denver. Intrigued, he followed my work, watching me on a podcast and quickly reading my first book, "White Flame," which chronicles my own metaphysical journey. Alan felt a strong connection to my experiences and insights, leading him to become a client of mine in the realm of Death and Spiritual Doula-ing.

The night after we met, Alan couldn't sleep. Guided by spirit, he felt an overwhelming urge to ask me to write his story. Coincidentally, I, too, felt a stirring in my spirit, an undeniable message that I needed to help him share his journey. It was as if the universe was orchestrating our collaboration, bringing us together to fulfill a greater purpose.

By telling Alan's story, we are marking a significant milestone off his soul contract before he departs this realm. As a Death Doula, I am dedicated to capturing his legacy, ensuring that his experiences and insights are preserved for future generations.

As a Spiritual Doula, I understand the soul's deep need to complete its contract, to fulfill its purpose, and to leave a lasting impact on the world.

Alan's story is one of hope, resilience, allowance, trust, and transformation. It is a testament to the power of spiritual awakening and the journey of becoming one's true self. Through his past life regressions, near-death experience, and encounters with the metaphysical, Alan has unearthed profound truths about his existence and purpose. His journey is a beacon of light for those navigating their own spiritual paths, offering guidance and inspiration.

As a published author, I have the necessary tools to pull Alan's story together, weaving his experiences into a cohesive narrative that captures the essence of his spiritual journey. This book is more than just a biography; it is a spiritual guide, a legacy, and a testament to the transformative power of spiritual awakening.

I invite you to embark on this journey with Alan, to explore the depths of his experiences, and to find inspiration in his story. May his journey of self-discovery and spiritual awakening resonate with you and encourage you to embrace your own path with hope, resilience, and trust.

With Love and Light,

Brianna Lafferty

Introduction

Alan Jones's life is a testament to the transformative power of spiritual awakening. Born into a lineage of resilience and perseverance, Alan's early years were shaped by the steadfast practicality and logical framework of his engineer's mind. However, his journey would lead him far beyond the confines of engineering, guiding him to embrace the profound depths of the spirit world.

Alan's childhood was rooted in the values of hard work and determination, inherited from his grandparents who established their lives in Escondido, California. His grandfather, John Wesley Jones, and grandmother, Ida Jones, epitomized the spirit of early pioneers, facing adversity head-on and building a life from the ground up. This foundation of strength and tenacity was further solidified by Alan's parents, whose unwavering dedication to family and community left an indelible mark on his character.

As a young man, Alan pursued a career in electrical engineering, a path that seemed preordained given his analytical prowess and methodical nature. His early professional life was marked by achievements and a growing sense of personal accomplishment. Yet, amidst the success and stability, Alan felt a persistent, gnawing emptiness—an unspoken longing for something beyond the material and tangible.

The turning point in Alan's life came with a series of serendipitous encounters and experiences that slowly unveiled the hidden layers of his spiritual self. These moments of awakening were both subtle and profound, nudging him towards a path of introspection and deeper understanding. His rigid worldview began to soften, making space for the mystical and the unknown.

Guided by his sense of allowance and help from others, Alan embarked on a journey of spiritual rebirth, akin to a caterpillar metamorphosing into a butterfly. This process was neither swift nor easy; it required Alan to confront his deepest fears and release long-held beliefs. Yet, with each step, he moved closer to a state of harmony and enlightenment, gradually aligning with his true, authentic self.

Throughout this journey, Alan's transformation was not just personal but profoundly spiritual. He learned to navigate the delicate balance between the physical and spiritual realms, finding solace and purpose in the interconnectedness of all things. His story serves as a beacon of hope and inspiration for those seeking to awaken their own spiritual selves, demonstrating that it is never too late to embrace the call of the spirit, and a testament to how real the spiritual world is.

As Alan prepares to return home, completing the final chapter of his soul contract, his story stands as a powerful guide to the enduring spirit of human transformation. His life, once defined by the precision of engineering, is now a symphony of spiritual wisdom and inner peace, a legacy that will inspire generations to come.

1

A Structured Beginning

A snapshot of Alan's life through items on his shelf
Alan Jones

Chapter 1

The Foundation of a Journey

Alan Jones's journey commenced in a humble setting, deeply rooted in the traditions and struggles of a family that valued hard work and resilience. Born at 3:47 AM on Tuesday, April 8, 1941, in Los Angeles, California, Alan was born into a family rooted in both resilience and perseverance. His grandparents, pioneers in their own right, had instilled a profound sense of determination in their descendants. This foundation prepared Alan for a life that would oscillate between the tangible realms of engineering and the ethereal domains of spirituality.

The first bridge between the 3D physical realm and that of the spiritual one, would be his baptism on January 3, 1943, at the Southern Presbyterian Church, by the pastor S. Martin Eiosath. While too young to understand the meaning behind the act, baptism in the Presbyterian faith, parents may reaffirm their faith in Jesus Christ, commit to nurturing their children in the church, and lead their children to accept Jesus Christ as Lord and Savior. Lightly put, this act is an introduction to the spiritual world in a sense.

A part of Alan's childhood that I find fascinating, possibly due to my age, is the small town in which he lived. In 1945 his father was working for the City of Los Angeles, Department of Water and Powerand was transferred to Silver Lake, California. Silver Lake was a small complex of six or eight houses which was north of Baker, California at a switching station on the high voltage power line that went from Hoover Dam on the Colorado River to Los Angeles. The town was so small that his mom had to drive him to the next town over for school where he made up the entirety of the 1st grade. As a child, he would not only explore the desert around him, but he also very much enjoyed his time at the switching station. He would analyze the large room that had a loud, consistent hum as it was filled with dials, gauges and controls. The isolated, desert lifestyle came pretty naturally to him and his parents, as his grandparents were self-sufficient when living on a farm, and the switching station would ignite his chosen career path later into life.

Chapter 2

The Seeds of Engineering

As Alan Jones entered his formative years in Compton, California, the foundation of his future as an engineer was being unwittingly laid through seemingly ordinary childhood activities. The move to Compton in 1948 marked a new chapter in Alan's life, characterized by vivid memories and hands-on experiences that sparked his curiosity and creativity.

One of the most poignant memories from this period was the building of a crystal radio. This wasn't just a pastime; it was a venture into the basics of electrical engineering. Alan constructed the radio by winding an inductor and pairing it with a variable capacitor for tuning. The crystal, touched delicately with a wire probe, became a tool for exploring the properties of radio signals. He extended a wire across the roof to serve as an antenna and connected a water pipe for grounding, marveling at how, on good nights, the radio captured clear signals from several stations. This experience was not only a demonstration of his budding technical skills but also a start into his ability to innovate with limited resources.

Alan's bedroom in Compton became a personal workshop where his engineering mindset flourished. Beyond the radio, he crafted a nightstand from an all-wood orange crate, demonstrating an early eye for design and functionality. He also indulged in building model planes and boats, primarily from balsa wood—a popular material before the advent of plastics. These models, including a seaplane and a World War II fighter plane, were meticulously assembled and varnished. Although he never flew the gas-powered model airplane he built, the process of assembling and testing the engine was a practical lesson in mechanics.

These childhood hobbies were more than just play; they were Alan's first forays into understanding and manipulating the physical world through engineering principles. Each model built and circuit created added layers to his understanding of how things worked, setting the stage for his later career. Even the toys and tools he longed for and eventually received, like the chemistry and erector sets, further expanded his technical acumen.

Alan's early exposure to engineering principles through recreational activities laid a robust foundation for his professional journey. The skills and interests cultivated during those early years in Compton were not just stepping stones but also the building blocks of his identity as an engineer. This phase of his life, rich with experimentation and discovery, highlighted the natural progression from playful curiosity to a serious career in electrical engineering, illustrating the seamless connection between childhood interests and adult vocations.

As Alan grew, so did his aptitude for logical thinking and problem-solving, leading him to pursue a career in engineering. His professional journey was marked by precision and analytical rigor—skills that earned him respect and success in his field. Yet, despite his accomplishments, there was an unfulfilled longing, a sense that something deeper was calling him.

Chapter 3

Life on Grandfather's Farm

From the time Alan was born until he went to college, he frequently visited his father's parents and brothers on his grandfather's farm in Escondido, California. These visits were a source of joy and learning for Alan, offering a break from city life and a chance to experience the rural lifestyle firsthand. The farm, spanning 160 acres, was initially a fully functional dairy farm, though it transitioned over the years as the dairy operations ceased, leaving a small barn where his grandfather continued to milk a few cows.

The farm was a playground for young Alan, filled with endless opportunities for adventure and learning.

He learned about farm animals, how to drive a tractor, and even got involved in house construction with his uncle. Horseback riding with his cousins and hunting rabbits in the fields near the hills at the back of the farm were some of his favorite activities.

One of Alan's vivid memories from the farm involved an incident with a post hole. He managed to get his knee stuck in the hole, requiring someone to come and lift him out. He was always fascinated by the cows and spent countless hours trying to get close to them, even attempting to ride them, though he never succeeded.

Alan also enjoyed digging up licorice plants in the apple orchard and chewing on their roots. He had an old magnet from an early model "T" car that he used to drag around the dirt driveway, collecting all kinds of metallic treasures, including many square nails used in the construction of his grandfather's house.

Alan's grandfather kept bees for honey, and Alan often accompanied him to care for the bees. He learned about the process of honey extraction and the use of smoke to calm the bees. His grandfather also taught him how to drive the farm's caterpillar tractor and his uncle's Ford tractor, skills that gave Alan a sense of responsibility and accomplishment.

The farm had various fascinating items, like the

milking suction cups from the dairy, which Alan loved to play with. The old house on the farm had a unique construction, with 2x3 framed outer walls and 1-inch thick interior walls made from 1x6 or 1x8 lumber. The bathroom and laundry room, added later, were accessible only from outside and were quite rudimentary, with no built-in heating and a simple electric heater to take the chill off.

Alan was fascinated by his grandfather's shaving tools, especially the razor and shaving brush used to create a lather from soap. He also remembers the brick building near the kitchen, used to store food, and later converted into a large walk-in freezer by his uncle.

Sleeping in the old farmhouse was an experience, with its thin walls and the presence of creatures like "Daddy long legs" spiders. His grandmother used to make butter with a large glass jar churn, and Alan loved the fresh buttermilk that resulted from the process.

Holidays were special times on the farm. Thanksgiving meals were grand affairs with tables laden with a variety of foods. One memorable Thanksgiving had the meal served outdoors on a long table covered with food. Christmas was marked by caroling to neighboring farms, a tradition Alan enjoyed immensely.

Hunting rabbits in the back fields was a regular

activity, and there were also encounters with large rattlesnakes. Alan recalls a dramatic moment when he spotted a snake, causing his uncle Francis to leap into the air in surprise. They managed to shoot the snake, but no one was willing to cook it.

The farm's water came from a well dug by Alan's grandfather, surrounded by bamboo. The living room housed an old upright piano and a hand-crank record player with a large horn speaker, adding to the rustic charm of the farmhouse.

When Alan's uncle Francis decided to build a new house on the farm, Alan got his first exposure to house construction. He helped with various tasks as the new house was built around the old one, which was eventually dismantled.

The farm life included seasonal activities like grunion hunting at Carlsbad beach, where they collected large sacks of grunion fish. They also went apple picking in Julian, California, and cherry picking in the Escondido area, adding to the rich tapestry of Alan's childhood memories.

Alan's mother, Virginia Lee Bruestle, was born in Ravenswood, West Virginia, and came from a diverse background with roots in Germany and Ireland. After her mother's death, Virginia moved west to Albuquerque, New Mexico, where she studied to become a secretary before eventually meeting Alan's father in California.

Alan's father, born near Escondido, California, helped on the dairy farm but chose not to continue its operations. He had a challenging youth, raised by his grandparents after the death of his father. Despite these hardships, Alan's father built a life in Escondido, contributing to the rich family history that Alan grew up appreciating.

The time Alan spent on his grandfather's farm was instrumental in shaping his early years. The farm was a place of learning, adventure, and deep family connections. These experiences not only provided Alan with practical skills and cherished memories but also laid the foundation for the values and resilience that would guide him throughout his life. The farm visits, the traditions, and the close-knit family environment left an indelible mark on Alan, influencing his outlook and personal growth as he moved into adulthood. Alan would later discover more about his intense connection to his grandfather and the farm when he learned more about his past lives.

Chapter 4

The Formative High School Years

In 1957, the Jones family moved to Independence, California, a small town nestled in the Owens Valley, at the eastern foot of the High Sierra mountains. This move marked a significant shift from city life to a more rural setting, where Alan's father worked on constructing power lines for the City of Los Angeles, Department of Water and Power. The change in environment presented both challenges and opportunities for Alan as he began attending Owens Valley High School.

Initially, Alan found it difficult to adjust to his new school, preferring to remain a loner. However, the friendly nature of the students at Owens Valley High soon drew him out of his shell. With a class size of only 13 students and a total high school population of about 50, Alan quickly became an active participant in school activities. He joined the school annual staff as a photographer, became the senior class treasurer, and even served as the timekeeper for basketball games.

Alan's role as the school photographer allowed him to delve deeply into photography, a hobby that would influence his later career. Using a "speed graphics" camera, he meticulously set up shots, focused images on the ground glass plate, and processed photos in the school's darkroom. This hands-on experience with photography honed his attention to detail and technical skills, which would later be crucial in his engineering endeavors.

Alan's interest in science was further fueled by his chemistry class. One memorable experiment involved making chlorine gas—an endeavor that resulted in Alan producing too much gas and having to step outside to clear his lungs. Despite the mishap, these experiments nurtured his curiosity and provided a solid foundation in scientific principles. Another experiment involved making candy, which demonstrated his ability to follow precise guidelines and achieve successful results, much like in his future engineering projects.

Also during his high school years, Alan's fascination with electronics grew. He spent countless hours building Heathkit products, assembling radios, and experimenting with various electronic circuits. One of his prized possessions was a shortwave radio, which he used to listen to distant broadcasts, honing his skills in signal reception and understanding radio frequencies. This practical experience was instrumental in developing his technical expertise and passion for electronic engineering.

These years were also marked by outdoor adventures and family trips. He enjoyed hunting and fishing in the Owens Valley, often exploring the valleys and deserts in search of Indian arrowheads and other treasures. Family camping trips into the High Sierra mountains fostered a deep appreciation for nature and self-sufficiency. These experiences enriched his understanding of the natural world and complemented his scientific interests.

Alan's first job at a local Richfield gas station introduced him to the working world. He learned to interact with customers and even picked up a new hobby—gemstone polishing—from his boss. This job not only provided practical skills but also taught him the value of hard work and perseverance.

During his years in Independence, Alan's growing

interest in electronics was unknowingly the beginning of his later spiritual awakening. Building and fixing radios and other electronic devices became more than a technical exercise; it was a form of exploration and discovery. The precision required in assembling Heathkit products and the satisfaction of creating functional devices mirrored the meticulous path he would later follow in his spiritual awakening. The patience and attention to detail learned through these projects were skills that would serve him well in his journey towards understanding the deeper, spiritual aspects of life.

Alan's high school years in Independence were a blend of academic pursuits, practical skills, and personal growth. These experiences laid a robust foundation for his future career as an electronic and aerospace engineer. The discipline and curiosity nurtured during this time were key elements in his professional development and later spiritual journey. The small town of Independence, with its tight community and vast natural beauty, provided the perfect backdrop for Alan to cultivate the skills and mindset that would define his remarkable life.

Chapter 5

College Days – A Path Unseen

In the spring of 1959, Alan Jones graduated from high school and spent the summer working at the local Richfield gas station before leaving home to attend the University of California, Berkeley. His journey to Berkeley was marked by a mix of excitement and apprehension, as he transitioned from the familiar environment of Independence, California, to the bustling campus life. Despite the initial shock of independence, Alan quickly adapted to his new surroundings and embraced the vibrant college experience.

Living in a student-operated off-campus dormitory, Alan immersed himself in the communal aspects of college life. He worked in the central kitchen as a dishwasher and eventually became the kitchen manager, coordinating meal preparations and managing the kitchen operations. This responsibility not only honed his organizational skills but also instilled a sense of independence and self-reliance.

During his second year at Berkeley, Alan learned surveying and spent his summers back in the High Sierra mountains, working as a surveyor. This experience, surrounded by the majestic and freeing nature of the mountains, provided him with a sense of serenity and connection to the natural world. The mountains, with their spiritual and liberating aura, subtly hinted at the deeper spiritual journey that awaited him, although at the time, Alan was primarily focused on his burgeoning engineering career and the odd sights that beheld him while there.

Alan's academic journey was not without its challenges. Struggling with his undergraduate courses, he sought guidance from the school counseling office, which helped him realize his aptitude for engineering. Deciding to transfer to California State Polytechnic College (Cal Poly) in San Luis Obispo, he effectively started his engineering education anew. Cal Poly's hands-on approach to learning proved to be the perfect fit for Alan, and he thrived in this practical environment.

At Cal Poly, Alan had his first exposure to digital computers with the Bendix G-15, which he learned to operate and program on his own. His project to find the square root of a number using assembly language marked the beginning of his deep dive into the world of computing. Cal Poly's emphasis on practical skills, including welding, machining, and sheet metal working, complemented his theoretical studies and prepared him for a career in electronic engineering.

Despite the rigorous academic schedule, Alan found time for social activities and pranks, which became a significant part of his college life. One memorable prank involved a small battery-powered FM transmitter built by his roommate, which they used to eavesdrop on conversations in the bathroom during a party. The girls, upon discovering the transmitter, were understandably furious yet forgiving, highlighting the mischievous, yet close camaraderie among Alan and his friends.

While Alan was not yet fully aware of the spiritual world around him, there were moments that hinted at this deeper connection. The freeing nature of the mountains where he surveyed during the summers, the serene beauty of the High Sierra, and the mystical experiences like the FM radio transmitter prank, subtly pointed towards a broader, unseen reality. However, at this stage, Alan's focus remained firmly on his engineering studies and career.

In 1965, after six years of college, Alan graduated

with a Bachelor of Science in Electronic Engineering. The transition from Berkeley to Cal Poly extended his education, but it also enriched his learning experience. His first job at AiResearch Manufacturing Company, a division of the Garrett Corporation, marked the beginning of his professional career. Although initially disappointed by a department change, Alan soon realized that his focus on computers was more aligned with his interests than circuit design and motor controllers.

The early days of his career involved designing analog computers with motors, gears, and cams, a process that required precision and a solid mathematical foundation. As digital technology advanced, Alan transitioned to working on small airborne digital computers, a shift that kept him at the forefront of technological innovation.

Alan's college years were a blend of rigorous academic pursuit, practical hands-on learning, and the carefree spirit of youth. While his focus was on establishing himself as an engineer, the experiences and subtle spiritual undercurrents of these years laid the groundwork for his future spiritual awakening. The mountains, the pranks, and the camaraderie all played a role in shaping the man who would later explore the depths of the spiritual world, even if the clues were only dimly perceived at the time.

Cal Poly College Friend Group
Alan Jones

Chapter 6

The Early Years of Marriage

On July 16, 1966, just a few years after meeting Coralie at college, Alan Jones and Coralie Silvey were married in Victorville, California. The ceremony, held in a Catholic church, was a beautiful affair marked by the presence of family and friends. Alan's long-time friend, Mike Sims, stood by his side as best man, proof of their enduring friendship since their days in Compton. The reception took place on the front lawn of Coralie's parents' home, and despite the playful antics of their friends filling their car with newspapers, Alan and Coralie's love and excitement for their future together shone through.

Their honeymoon was spent in the serene isolation of an architect's home in the mountains north of Los Angeles. This week-long retreat provided the newlyweds with the perfect opportunity to bond and enjoy each other's company away from the hustle and bustle of everyday life.

After their honeymoon, Alan and Coralie settled into a two-bedroom apartment in Torrance, California. It was a modest start, but their shared enthusiasm for building a life together made the apartment feel like a true home. Alan even began constructing a Cutty Sark ship model, a project that symbolized his meticulous nature and love for craftsmanship.

In 1967, they moved to a rental house in Lakewood, California, to be closer to Coralie's school, Cal State at Long Beach. Alan's career took a significant turn when he was asked to deliver computer units to Italy. Seizing the opportunity, he surprised Coralie by showing up at her class to take passport photos, and soon they were off on an adventure that took them through Italy, Switzerland, Belgium, and England. This trip not only broadened their horizons but also brought them closer together as they navigated foreign lands and languages.

Despite the joy and excitement of their early years, Alan and Coralie faced challenges. Coralie was deeply spiritual and immersed in the metaphysical world, often surrounded by friends who were psychics, tarot readers, and open to unseen realms. Alan, however, was skeptical of these "woo-woo" activities and often made himself scarce when her friends visited. This difference in their beliefs was an early strain on their marriage, with Alan even debating whether to allow some of Coralie's friends into their home. These early tensions would later prove to be a blessing in disguise as Alan confronted his own spiritual battles.

Alan and Coralie's life was filled with memorable adventures and travels. During their trip to Italy, they visited a monastery high on a mountain, where they met a young American soon to be ordained as a priest. This encounter was a highlight, showcasing the blend of spirituality and exploration that marked their travels. In Geneva, they attended a Garrett office party on a boat and spent Christmas Eve enjoying a Yule log cake and Christmas lights in their hotel room.

Driving in Europe presented its own set of challenges and memorable moments, from navigating the chaotic traffic in Italy to running out of gas in France and relying on sign language to communicate. Each destination, whether it was the majestic cathedral in Milano or the bustling streets of Brussels, added to the rich adventure of their early married life.

In 1968, Alan and Coralie bought their first home in Long Beach, California. It was an older house that required significant work, but they approached the task with energy and enthusiasm. Alan's engineering skills came to the fore as he took on major remodeling projects, learning plumbing, electrical work, and carpentry in the process. The house became a symbol of their hard work and determination, and it was here that their two sons were born.

Alan's career continued to flourish as he worked on various projects and attended graduate courses to further his knowledge. Meanwhile, Coralie's spiritual interests remained a constant, quietly influencing their household even as Alan focused on more tangible pursuits. Despite his initial resistance to her metaphysical world, the seeds of spiritual awareness were subtly being planted.

The couple's social life was vibrant, filled with parties, outings, and community activities. They went on clam digging trips, attended Christmas parties at the Shrine Auditorium, and enjoyed private evenings at Disneyland courtesy of Garrett's corporate events. Alan also supported their sons in youth soccer and scouting, actively participating in their activities and fostering a strong family bond.

While the early years of their marriage were marked by Alan's skepticism towards Coralie's spiritual world, these experiences laid the groundwork for his eventual spiritual awakening. The strain caused by their differing beliefs tested their relationship, but it also prepared Alan for the spiritual journey that lay ahead. Coralie's unwavering faith and the presence of her spiritual friends would later become invaluable as Alan faced his own spiritual challenges.

Alan and Coralie's early years of marriage were a blend of joy, adventure, and challenges. Their love and commitment to each other helped them navigate the initial strains of their differing worldviews. Little did Alan know that the very aspects of Coralie's life he resisted would become crucial in his journey towards spiritual enlightenment. The foundation they built during these years, characterized by love, perseverance, and mutual respect, set the stage for the profound transformation that awaited them both. His marriage was not just a union of hearts but also of spirits. Together with his wife, he navigated the complexities of life, balancing career demands with personal aspirations. Their journey was punctuated by joyous moments and trials that tested and ultimately strengthened their bond.

Chapter 7

Life as an Engineer

Alan Jones's journey as an engineer began even before he graduated, working as a summer hire in the lab at Garrett AiResearch. One of his early tasks involved testing electronic modules for the Blackbird, a top-secret plane capable of supersonic speeds, developed by Lockheed. It was a fascinating and highly classified project, and the existence of the Blackbird was only revealed to the public many years later.

After graduation, Alan joined Garrett full-time, though in a different department than initially expected. He was placed in the Air Data Computer Department, working on large mechanical computers that used cams, shaped potentiometers, motors, and gears for calculations. Despite his degree in Electronic

Engineering, Alan quickly adapted to the mechanical nature of these projects. His first major assignment was designing mechanical cams for the Air Data Computer used in the F-4 fighter plane, utilizing the IBM 7090 computer system for these designs.

Alan's role expanded to include gear design and atmospheric data calculations, essential for the high-altitude flights of military aircraft. He also developed a resistive element to measure outside air temperature and aircraft speed, showcasing his ability to bridge electronic and mechanical engineering disciplines.

As Alan's expertise grew, he was given his own Air Data Computer project for the Italian G91-Y aircraft. This role required coordinating all phases of design, working closely with both mechanical and electrical engineers. His work eventually took him to Italy, where he assisted customers in understanding the computer's construction and functionality. This international experience further aided in his growing reputation and skill in the field.

In the late 1960s, Alan was involved in pioneering projects to develop digital cockpit instruments for the DC-9 aircraft. Despite some reliability issues, these early forays into digital technology were crucial stepping stones for future innovations.

The early 1970s marked the beginning of Alan's

work with digital systems. He worked on a controller for the C-5 aircraft's landing gear, a project that required redesigning to compensate for mechanical limitations. This controller was one of the first digital systems Alan encountered, operating with discrete digital components before the advent of microprocessors.

As microprocessors began to emerge, Alan's department developed a proprietary 20-bit processor tailored for aircraft cockpit computations. Alan enjoyed the challenge of working with limited resources, writing and developing software often at the binary level. The compilers for these early systems ran on large mainframe computers, and programming required a deep understanding of both hardware and software.

Alan's ingenuity shone through in several unique projects. He designed a voltage regulator for a missile power supply system, which had to operate in the extreme environment of a jet engine combustion chamber. Another project involved creating a ground-based data acquisition system for collecting telemetry data from test missiles, demonstrating his versatility and technical prowess.

For a brief period, Alan took on a management role, overseeing a team of engineers working on a compass calibrator for aircraft. However, he found the political and corporate aspects of management unfulfilling and eventually returned to a senior technical position. In this role, he coordinated the writing of a complex software specification for the DC-10 Air Data Computer and designed an automated production test controller using an HP9000 computer.

Alan's engineering career was marked by a series of significant projects and innovations. From his early days testing modules for secretive military aircraft to leading complex digital system designs, Alan's journey was one of constant learning and adaptation. His ability to navigate both mechanical and electronic engineering realms made him a valuable asset in the aerospace industry. This period of his life laid a strong foundation for his later spiritual awakening, demonstrating the depth and versatility that characterized his professional and personal growth.

Chapter 8

A New Beginning in Albuquerque

After 15 years at Garrett AiResearch, where Alan Jones advanced from an entry-level engineer to an Engineering Specialist, he began feeling the urge for a change. The routine of the aerospace world had started to wear on him, and he sensed that it was time to move on. In 1981, when an opportunity arose with Sperry's new facility in Albuquerque, New Mexico, Alan saw it as a fresh start. He and Coralie discussed the move, and with mutual enthusiasm, they decided to relocate, hoping to provide their sons with the experience of country living.

In Albuquerque, they found a house in Corrales, situated on an acre of land. Although the house was a bit beyond their budget, they believed it was the perfect place for their family. The rural setting allowed their sons to experience the joys of country life, despite the financial challenges it brought. The move to Corrales marked a period of growth and bonding for the family, with Alan spending valuable time with his boys, learning to ski and engaging in outdoor activities.

Alan's introduction to skiing came with its share of struggles, but he persisted, taking lessons at the Sandia Crest ski area and eventually enjoying the sport. The boys took to skiing quickly, often leaving Alan to ski on his own. This led to many solo skiing adventures, which Alan enjoyed. His commitment to physical fitness grew, and by 1987, he was actively participating in long-distance cycling events and hiking the challenging trails of the Sandia Mountains.

By 1990, Alan was feeling burned out from the high-tech world of aerospace engineering. He and Coralie began discussing starting their own business, exploring various options until they landed on printing. They looked at a print business for sale in Durango, Colorado, but it wasn't viable. Their search for a letterpress led them to Peter Wells in Sandia Park, New Mexico. Peter had a complete print shop for sale, and Alan and Coralie decided to buy it, moving the business to Taos, New Mexico.

Unbeknownst to Alan, the printing press would become a central part of his spiritual journey. Initially drawn to it for practical reasons, Alan later discovered deeper, more spiritual connections to this endeavor. The process of working with the printing press awakened something within him that would eventually lead him to explore aspects of spiritual self. One significant revelation was his past involvement with the book *Rabble in Arms*, which profoundly affected him when he merely touched it. This connection to the past began to unravel the mysteries of his spiritual path.

Moving to Taos brought its own set of challenges. Their house in Corrales didn't sell as quickly as they hoped, forcing them to auction it and lose their equity. Despite the financial setback, they established their printing business in Taos. The business provided a modest income and a sense of fulfillment for Alan, who found joy in the work, reminiscent of his early fascination with printing in junior high school.

The years in Taos were marked by a mix of professional satisfaction and financial struggle. Although the printing business was never a big moneymaker, it allowed Alan to step away from the high-pressure environment of aerospace engineering. The change in career was timely, aligning with his growing interest in spiritual matters and providing the mental space to explore new directions in life.

One day, while working in the shop, a woman came

in and asked him how he was doing. Alan's usual response of "I'm fine" turned into a heartfelt "Better than fine!" as a wave of intense love washed over him. The woman then wanted to buy a postcard, and as Alan wondered how she would pay for it, she seemingly pulled the money out of thin air. As she left, she mentioned, "My daughter, Destiny, will be by later." Sure enough, Destiny would appear at Alan's doorstep, although not in human form as he expected.

As Alan settled into his new life, the spiritual aspects of his journey became more pronounced. His initial attraction to the printing press and the deeper connections he uncovered were just the beginning. Alan's past lives and the spiritual significance of his experiences began to reveal themselves, leading him on a path of profound self-discovery. The purchase of the printing press, a seemingly practical decision, turned out to be a pivotal moment in his spiritual birth story.

Chapter 9

The Journey to Scotland

Alan's journey to spiritual awakening and rebirth found a significant chapter in his travels to Scotland. This trip, deeply intertwined with moments of reflection, solitude, and historical exploration, catalyzed a shift in his spiritual consciousness and opened new doors to understanding himself and his past.

In October 1997, Alan and Coralie embarked on a six-week journey to Scotland, staying in various bed and breakfasts and small hotels. Each place offered a new perspective and a chance for Alan to explore not only the land but also his inner self. The trip was intended to provide them both with a much-needed respite from their busy lives in Taos, New Mexico, and to immerse themselves in the rich history and serene landscapes of Scotland.

One of the first reflections Alan had was the profound quiet and peace that Scotland offered. In Birsay, despite initial struggles to find solitude, Alan began to appreciate the time apart from Coralie. This separation allowed him to reflect deeply, something he felt he could not do amidst the constant demands of daily life back home. The quiet nights and the cold winds by the sea provided a perfect backdrop for this introspection.

As they traveled through the Orkney Islands, visiting historical sites like the Italian Chapel and the Ring of Brodgar, Alan felt a deep connection to the ancient history of the land. The historical richness of Scotland resonated with him, offering a contrast to his life back in the United States. This historical immersion was not just an educational experience but also a spiritual one. The standing stones and ancient ruins seemed to whisper stories of the past, invoking a sense of continuity and timelessness in Alan's mind.

One particularly enlightening moment came during a visit to the standing stones of Callanish. Guided by Margaret Curtis, an archaeologist, Alan learned about the stones' historical and mythological significance. This visit was more than just a tour; it felt like a bridge to a distant past, stirring memories and feelings that

Alan couldn't quite place at the time but would later recognize as connections to his own spiritual journey.

Throughout the trip, Alan often found himself in solitude, contemplating his life, his choices, and his future. He frequently wrote about the need to find direction and purpose, questioning his career, his relationships, and his personal goals. The peaceful yet powerful landscapes of Scotland provided a perfect setting for this internal dialogue. Alan's reflections during this time laid the groundwork for his spiritual rebirth, a process that would unfold more clearly as he continued his journey.

One significant story from the trip was a dream Alan had, where he found himself with the power to move objects with his mind. This dream, though fantastical, symbolized his growing realization of the potential within himself, a potential that he had not fully recognized or tapped into until this journey.

The trip also had practical implications. Alan and Coralie discussed their business, contemplating changes that would allow them more personal freedom. They considered phasing out their printing business and focusing on ventures that would enable them to pursue their interests without the constraints of a strict schedule. This reflection was crucial, as it signaled Alan's desire to align his work more closely with his newfound spiritual insights and personal aspirations.

While in Scotland, Alan felt an inexplicable draw to certain places and historical artifacts. This attraction hinted at deeper connections, possibly linked to past lives. Alan's trip to Scotland was more than a vacation; it was a transformative journey that played a crucial role in his spiritual awakening and rebirth. The serene landscapes, the historical depth, and the reflective solitude provided a perfect backdrop for Alan to explore his inner self and his spiritual connections. This journey laid the foundation for the profound spiritual discoveries that would follow, marking Scotland as a pivotal chapter in Alan's life.

2

Spiritual Awakening: The Turning Point

Alan's Dream Journal - a Testament to his Journey
Alan Jones

Chapter 10

The Journey Begins

Alan's journey toward spiritual awakening began in the late 1990s, a time when he had lost touch with his Presbyterian roots and had distanced himself from any form of organized religion. Despite this detachment, a series of experiences gradually unfolded, leading him toward a profound transformation.

One day in particular, while working in his store, Alan noticed a yellow glow surrounding an employee's body. Initially attributing it to an illusion of sunlight, he soon realized that he was witnessing something beyond his understanding – an aura. This isolated event was the first of many that challenged his perception of reality.

Approximately two years later, another inexplicable incident occurred. A customer entered the store, exchanged pleasantries with Alan, and mentioned that her daughter, Destiny, would visit later. Although no one named Destiny appeared, Alan was left with an overwhelming sense of euphoria and a lingering question about the true nature of the encounter. Was the woman an angel or spirit in human form? This event left a lasting imprint on Alan's memory and would recount this many times looking back on the events leading up to his spiritual awakening. He would come to realize that “Destiny” was not a woman, but fate all along.

Chapter 11

Four Gates

In early 2002, Alan began to experience dreams that would later manifest as reality. Initially skeptical, he could no longer deny the accuracy and frequency of these precognitive dreams. These experiences marked the beginning of a significant shift in his understanding of reality and consciousness.

As Alan delved deeper into his spiritual journey, he began to experience more frequent and vivid bleed-throughs between his physical reality and the spiritual realms. These moments of convergence manifested as fleeting visions, intuitive insights, and profound sensations of déjà vu, where past lives, other dimensions, and alternate timelines seemed to intersect with his present consciousness. Alan found himself increasingly aware of the thin veil separating his material existence from the vast, interconnected spiritual tapestry beyond. These bleed-throughs offered glimpses of his soul's expansive journey across time and space, re-affirming the interconnectedness of all life and the profound spiritual truths that underlie our everyday reality..

As these experiences intensified, Alan sought guidance from Patricia Padilla, a medical intuitive. Although initially hesitant, his sessions with Patricia opened his mind to the possibilities of the unseen world. Patricia advised him to observe his experiences without becoming personally involved, but Alan found it difficult to remain detached.

One of the most transformative experiences occurred during a Shamanic journey meeting. Alan found himself in a trance, vividly experiencing the process of giving birth. Although unsettling, this experience symbolized a spiritual rebirth, marking a significant milestone in his journey.

As Alan delved deeper into his spiritual awakening, he began to question the nature of reality itself. The clear distinctions he once held began to blur, leading him to explore various philosophies and teachings. He learned about the illusion of reality, often referred to as Maya, and the concept that the physical world is a construct of the mind.

Through his explorations, Alan discovered that

his experiences were part of a broader spectrum of human consciousness. He read extensively about altered states of consciousness, lucid dreaming, and the works of Carl Jung and Stephen LaBerge. These studies provided a framework for understanding his experiences and integrating them into his life.

Alan's journey of spiritual awakening was marked by a series of profound experiences that challenged his perception of reality and led him toward a deeper understanding of consciousness. From seeing auras and experiencing precognitive dreams to undergoing multiple rebirths and other worldly experiences, Alan's path was set to one of continuous exploration and growth.

Chapter 12

The Unveiling of New Realities

Alan's spiritual journey began in a rather unexpected manner, during a period of self-discovery and exploration. His first significant encounter with the spiritual world happened in 2002 while he was at his store, Sage Papers. One afternoon, he was visiting his friend Bonnie when he suddenly saw a yellow aura around her. Initially, Alan thought the sunlight was playing tricks on his eyes, but no matter how he moved, the aura remained.

Around the same time, Alan had a vivid dream about someone renting his old space at Yucca Plaza. A few days later, he discovered that this dream was a premonition, as a new business had indeed moved into that space. These events were unsettling yet intriguing for

Alan, pushing him to question the nature of reality and his perception of it.

During a trip in early 2002, Alan's perception of reality was further challenged when he visited the Santa Fe Trail. While standing on a quiet road in Eastern New Mexico, he experienced what felt like a reenactment of the trail's history. He saw and heard the sounds of wagons, horses, and people moving along the trail as if he had stepped back in time. This clairvoyant experience made Alan realize he was tapping into energies and memories that lingered in certain place.

In the fall of 2002, Alan's journey took a decisive turn when he met Patricia Padilla, a curandera (healer). Patricia's insights and healing methods opened new doors for Alan. During their first session, Patricia sensed that Alan had an encounter with extraterrestrials when he was six years old. Although initially skeptical, Alan found himself releasing intense emotions during an acupuncture session called the "Four Gates" with Patricia. This emotional release felt similar to a sexual orgasm, marking the beginning of a profound transformation.

Chapter 13

The Spiritual Rebirth

Alan's journey continued with a series of profound experiences that he described as a spiritual rebirth. One day, he felt a sudden urge to take a warm salt and soda bath, during which he experienced shedding his old self like a snake shedding its skin. In this state, Alan was overcome as a woman named Ellen, who was pregnant with a new version of himself. This transformation was intense and disorienting, leading Alan to question his sanity at times. The intensity of the emotions, the rebirth, and the mental images often had Alan crying on the kitchen floor. Coralie, who was much more in tune with the spiritual phenomena would comfort him and let him know that these were real occurrences and not that of his mind. His physical guide, Patricia, would also be a reassuring and calming voice on the other end of the phone line, even though at first, he blamed her for putting a hex on him. However, he would eventually realize that he was undergoing a rebirth, shedding his old identity and embracing a new one.

The rebirth of Ellen marked the first of two significant transformations in Alan's spiritual journey. Ellen's rebirth was a profound moment of awakening, shedding old layers of identity and embracing a renewed sense of purpose and spiritual clarity. This pivotal transformation laid the groundwork for what was to come. The second rebirth, however, was Alan's own metamorphosis, an even deeper and more encompassing shift. This subsequent rebirth saw Alan integrating the lessons and experiences of his past lives, spiritual insights, and metaphysical explorations. It was a complete transformation, birthing a new Alan—one who was not only awakened but also fully aligned with his authentic, spiritual self. This new Alan embodied a higher state of consciousness, reflecting the culmination of his soul's journey and his readiness to fulfill his ultimate purpose with grace, wisdom, and compassion.

Dream Class Painting Named "Scream"
Alan Jones

Chapter 14

Past Lives and Memory Regression

Alan's exploration of rebirth and spiritual awakening would only deepen after his acupuncture session with Patricia and the following embodiment of Ellen. Alan developed a new, unquenchable thirst for knowledge of the spiritual realm that laid just beyond this one. He would dive into some of his many past lives through a variety of means, meditation circles, dreams, past life regressions, and oftentimes the memories would bleed through the veil into his waking life.

Alan's exploration of past lives was first inspired after his visit to Urquhart Castle in Scotland in 1997. The Isle of Orkney, with its familiar and comfortable aura, hinted at a deeper connection to the past. His journey into past lives truly began in earnest when he started experiencing vivid and detailed recollections.

During one such session, Alan found himself as a knight and king's guard in England, serving two kings. This vision came to him in a hypnagogic state, where he vividly felt the presence of a forest, the cool morning air, and the weight of chain mail. He took time to look at his helmet which had leather straps to sit upon his head. He made note that his sword sat on his right hip and that meant he was left handed at the time.The memory of a woman wearing a tall, conical headdress, also known as a Hennin, with a veil further anchored this experience in the 15th century.

Another significant recollection was of a man drowning, trapped under an iron plate at the bottom of a river, possibly related to an inability to swim face-down in this life. The plate was painted white and had large rivets. It appeared to be a piece of boiler from a river boat from a boiler explosion. This memory surfaced during a class with Gary Cooke at the University of New Mexico, highlighting the intense physical and emotional connections between past and present experiences.

Circling back to the printing press earlier in Alan’s life, the printing press played a pivotal role in Alan's spiritual journey. During a visit to the Taos library, he touched a book titled "Rabble in Arms" and was immediately thrown into an altered state of consciousness. He wandered through the library in a trance, unaware of his actions until he found himself at home, holding the book. This experience, combined with a psychic reading, revealed that Alan had been an underground printer involved in the political movements before America's independence. The deep affinity he felt for old printing presses and his eventual purchase of one for his business in Taos seemed predestined, connecting him to this significant past life.

Alan's journey through his past lives brought him full circle to a realization that helped define his strong attachment to his grandfather and his grandfather's farm. This connection was not just rooted in his current life but had deep, spiritual ties to his past incarnations. One of the most profound past life experiences revealed to Alan involved his great-grandmother, Martha Ann Jones.

In one session, Alan had a vivid vision of a woman lying under an Irishman as he made love to her. Guided by his regression therapist, Patricia, it was suggested that this woman could have been his great-grandmother Martha. This connection to Martha was further solidified in another session where Alan recalled a traumatic event. In this vision, he was a woman lying on a bare, rough wood floor, being beaten by a man who seemed drunk or angry. The intense emotions and physical sensations Alan experienced during this session left a lasting impact, making him realize his strong aversion to men who harm their wives. The pain and suffering he endured in that lifetime seemed to echo into his present life, influencing his perceptions and emotions.

Another memory that surfaced was of a woman in a coffin at her funeral. Alan found himself in a hypnopompic state, tracing his life back to birth when he suddenly envisioned himself lying in a lined cloth coffin. He explored the inside of the coffin and noticed that it was open to a room full of people dressed in black, mourning the woman's death. This vision was somber and deeply moving, adding another layer to his understanding of Martha's life and death.

These past life experiences were not merely random memories but pivotal moments that connected Alan to his current life in profound ways. The realization that he had once been Martha, his great-grandmother, helped explain his deep attachment to his grandfather and the farm where he spent his childhood. The farm, a place of fond memories and familial love, was a significant part of his life because it was tied to his past life experiences as Martha. It was another full circle realization, showing how intertwined his soul's journey was with his family's history.

Growing up, Alan had always felt a strong bond with

his grandfather and the farm. He learned about farm animals, how to drive a tractor, and even house construction while helping his uncle. These experiences were not just enjoyable but deeply fulfilling, giving him a sense of purpose and belonging. The farm was a place of learning and growth, where he connected with nature and family.

As Martha, Alan had endured hardships and trauma, but those experiences had also shaped his soul's resilience and strength. The love and connection he felt towards his grandfather's farm were a continuation of the deep familial ties that had spanned across lifetimes. This realization brought Alan a sense of peace and understanding, knowing that his bond with his family and the farm was part of a much larger spiritual journey.

Through these past life memories, Alan learned that the challenges and connections we experience in our current lives are often deeply rooted in our soul's history. Understanding these connections can bring healing and clarity, helping us to navigate our present lives with greater awareness and compassion. Alan's experiences serve as a reminder that our spiritual journeys are interconnected with those of our ancestors and that the love and lessons we share with our family are eternal.

Chapter 15

Shamanic Journeys and Spiritual Encounters

Alan's spiritual exploration extended to shamanic journeys and sessions with various psychics and healers. During a shamanic journey, he experienced the life of a primitive woman giving birth on a stone table, surrounded by hooded figures. Alan's commitment to exploring his spiritual path led him to engage in memory regression exercises. These sessions allowed him to delve deeper into his subconscious, uncovering more past lives and the lessons they held. From a priest in medieval times to a woman in a 19th-century farmhouse, each memory provided valuable insights into his soul's journey and its purpose.

During another powerful shamanic journey, Alan visited the Hall of Records, a mystical place where all knowledge and memories are stored. In this sacred space, he accessed information about his past lives and soul's purpose. The Hall of Records provided Alan with profound insights into his spiritual path, reinforcing his belief in the interconnectedness of all life and the continuity of the soul's journey through time.

He also encountered lives as a healer on the Santa Fe Trail, a Greek Orthodox priest, and a monk in Atlantis, among many others throughout his continual exploration of past life regressions. Brian Weiss states, “We are immortal. We will always be together.” This is the same message as Bruce Lipton learned from his study of the cell. From this and the message above about coexistence this implies that we will be together somewhere other than this earth plane. Somewhere on another plane or in another dimension.

Alan also ventured into the world of Astrology. This provided profound insights into Alan's spiritual awakening. A reading by Cat Moon in 2005 highlighted a major shift in his life, marked by the crossing of Uranus into his ascendant sign. This period was predicted to be a time of significant self-discovery and psychic vision. Alan was encouraged to embrace his mystical qualities and let go of old patterns. This astrological guidance affirmed the changes Alan was experiencing and provided a framework for understanding his spiritual evolution.

Other readings would provide more clues into his life, current and past, but another notable reading involved ET's (Extraterrestrial Beings.) As a child living in Silver Lake, he had experiences of being taken aboard a craft by visitors. These encounters introduced him to advanced knowledge and consciousness, which profoundly impacted him. The memories of these visits resurfaced later in life, adding another dimension to his spiritual understanding. These experiences underscored the theme of interconnectedness and the existence of higher realms of consciousness.

Each session provided fragments of his past, weaving a complex picture of experiences and lessons that shaped his spiritual awakening highlighting the intense physical and emotional experiences of past lives and their lingering impact on the present.

Chapter 16

Beyond Time – A Multidimensional Journey

In understanding his spiritual awakening, Alan came to realize that his past life regressions were not merely memories of bygone eras but rather reflections of his multidimensional self. Through various experiences and teachings, he grasped a profound truth: there is no linear time as we traditionally perceive it. Instead, everything exists in a state of dynamic energy and patterns, transcending the conventional notion of past, present, and future.

Alan's regression experiences, such as being a knight or a fortune teller, were not isolated events relegated to history. These lives were extensions of his greater, multidimensional being. Each life, each experience, was a facet of his vast existence, influencing and shaping who he was in the present moment. From the perspective of his three-dimensional, time-bound existence, these regressions appeared as past lives. However, in the broader scope of his spiritual reality, they were simultaneous dimensions of one cohesive being.

One insightful teaching came from Henry Bolduc's book, where a channeled entity named Pretty Flower offered wisdom about the nature of existence. Pretty Flower described herself as a combination of energies, emphasizing that she, like all beings, existed as a collection of vibrations that transcended specific moments in time. This understanding helped Alan see his past lives not as separate and distinct periods but as interconnected dimensions of his soul's journey.

Pretty Flower's teachings encouraged a shift in perspective. While it was useful for Alan to think of his past lives in the context of linear time to make sense of his experiences, he began to understand that all these lives were occurring simultaneously. This concept was akin to viewing his lives as overlays on tracing paper, each influencing the others in a complex, interwoven pattern.

This realization had profound implications for Alan's spiritual journey. It meant that his experiences as a knight, a fortune teller, or any other persona were not confined to the past. They were living, breathing aspects of his current existence, each dimension pulsating with energy and continuously interacting with his present life.

In practical terms, this understanding allowed Alan to draw on the strengths, lessons, and wisdom of his other lives in a more immediate and impactful way. He could access the courage of the knight, the intuitive insight of the fortune teller, and the resilience of his many other personas, integrating these qualities into his daily life.

As Alan embraced this multidimensional view of his existence, he found a deeper connection to his past, his present, and his future. He recognized that the emotional and spiritual growth he experienced in this life was mirrored and amplified across all dimensions of his being. This holistic approach to his spiritual awakening brought him a sense of wholeness and interconnectedness, reinforcing the idea that every aspect of his existence was valuable and essential to his overall journey.

Alan's journey of spiritual awakening and past life regression taught him that his soul's evolution was a continuous, multidimensional process. By embracing the timeless nature of his experiences, he was able to live more fully and authentically, drawing on the wisdom and energy of his entire being. This perspective not only enriched his spiritual path but also offered comfort and guidance to others navigating their own journeys of self-discovery and growth.

Chapter 17

Near-Death Experience

In many cultures and spiritual traditions, it is believed that significant life changes can be triggered by the act of cutting one's hair or beard. The beard, often seen as a symbol of wisdom, strength, and identity, holds profound personal and cultural significance. For Alan, the decision to cut his beard was not just a physical change, but the catalyst for a powerful spiritual awakening that would transform his life in unimaginable ways.

Alan had worn a beard for many years. It had become an integral part of his identity, a physical manifestation of his journey and experiences. However, in 2010 a few years into the spiritual awakening process, Alan felt a compelling urge to shave it off.

This decision was not taken lightly, as he intuitively sensed that this act would usher in a new phase of his life.

On the day he decided to cut his beard, Alan felt a mix of apprehension and anticipation. As the razor moved through the coarse hair, he felt as though he was shedding not just the beard, but layers of his old self.

The change was immediate and profound. Alan felt a change in energy, although he didn't understand the organization of the change. It was as though the act of cutting his beard had unlocked a door to a deeper part of himself. This newfound energy manifested in a heightened sensitivity to the spiritual world, and Alan began to experience an array of mystical phenomena.

Shortly after this transformative act, Alan found himself in a series of situations that further propelled his spiritual awakening. He noticed an increase in vivid dreams, and spiritual encounters and experiences.

With his beard gone, Alan felt exposed and vulnerable, yet also more open and receptive to the spiritual realms. He would begin attending workshops, meeting with spiritual teachers, and diving into books on subjects ranging from quantum mechanics to ancient mysticism.

A crucial moment in Alan's journey was his near-death experience (NDE). During this profound event, he felt an overwhelming sense of love and connection to the universe. This NDE solidified his belief in the continuity of the soul and the interconnectedness of all lives. The insights gained from this experience deepened his understanding of his past lives and their relevance to his current existence.

As the year drew to a close, Alan and Coralie decided to buy a new built-in oven for their kitchen. During the installation, Alan sprained his back, which led to sleepless nights in a reclining chair in the living room. Despite Coralie's advice to keep his legs elevated, he ignored her suggestion. This turned out to be a mistake, as a blood clot formed in his leg. One morning, after using the bathroom, Alan felt an intuitive sense that something was wrong. With no pain or other sensations, he asked Coralie to call 911.

Coralie, still groggy from sleep, took her time and used the bathroom before calling 911 from the landline. Alan remained calm, almost detached, as he waited. He might have been fading in and out of consciousness because he had no memory of the paramedics' arrival. He vaguely recalled being put on a gurney and noticing the cold winter morning as they took him to the ambulance.

The ambulance ride was a blur. Alan remembered

arriving at the hospital and then found himself out of his body, observing the paramedics and hospital staff transferring his body to a hospital bed. He saw them lift his body using a turquoise sheet from the ambulance gurney. The next thing he noticed was a pair of scissors beginning to cut his pants off before everything went black.

Alan's consciousness then shifted to a windowless, doorless tiled room. There was no body, only his awareness. The room had golden-brown tiles with darker brown stripes, and a hole in the center of the floor puzzled him. He occasionally heard a sound reminiscent of hundreds of soldiers marching. Eventually, the walls of the room crumbled, revealing an open sky and a distant, ominous black cloud. Alan realized this was serious but felt no panic, only a knowing.

In the next moment, Alan found himself in total darkness, sensing the presence of others nearby—points of consciousness exuding love and compassion. He understood he was between life and death and needed to decide whether to return to his body. With a mental checklist of his life contract items, he concluded that he had completed enough and chose not to go back. Disappointed by the absence of the expected tunnel of light, he resolved to stay in the darkness, seeing a string of unknown symbols moving across it.

Alan then awoke four days later, in a large hospital intensive care room, which seemed more like a grand space meant for families of patients with little chance of survival. The doctors later told him that his survival odds were less than 10%, with one doctor even asserting a 0% chance.

While he was in the darkness, Alan's heart had stopped three times due to a blood clot that had moved to his heart. The ER staff managed to restart his heart each time, but the clot eventually lodged in the artery between his heart and lungs, causing a massive pulmonary embolism. The ER doctor wanted to use an experimental drug to dissolve the clot, but he needed Coralie's consent. Initially hesitant, she ultimately signed the form because Alan had asked her to call 911.

After the clot was cleared, Alan was airlifted to a hospital in Albuquerque, New Mexico, better equipped for his recovery. He remained in a coma and on life support until he woke up on Wednesday. During his coma, his son noticed his hand moving as if wanting to write. With paper and pen provided by the nurses, Alan wrote eight pages of responses to questions. His notes included, "I Love all of you," "I would like to die now," and "Any questions?" The writing was not a conscious act but rather an automatic one from the other place of darkness.

These notes led to the decision to take Alan off life support. When the doctor removed the breathing tube, Alan was breathing on his own. Upon waking, he animatedly recounted his near-death experience, surprising the medical staff with his lucidity. The doctor called the ER doctor who first treated Alan, allowing them to speak briefly to join in the perplexing nature of his miraculous return to consciousness.

Weeks later, as Alan joked with the staff in his hometown doctor's office, a doctor who had helped revive him saw him in the hall and was astonished at his vibrant recovery. Alan's near-death experience marked a significant turning point, further deepening his spiritual journey and understanding of life beyond the physical realm.

Dots

Dots

I am a dot
Just a speck
What did you expect

I am a dot
A round what
Maybe a splot

I am a dot
Getting very large soon
You may call me moon

I am a dot
Come close
see me large

I am a dot
go far
see me small

I am a dot

-Alan Jones *creative writing for kids workshop*

Chapter 18

Embracing the New Reality and Sharing Wisdom

As Alan continued his spiritual exploration, he began to integrate his newfound knowledge and experiences into his daily life. He read extensively on topics like psychology, consciousness, quantum mechanics, and near-death experiences, seeking a scientific understanding of his spiritual encounters. Alan's journey was not without challenges, as he faced dark energies and negative emotions that surfaced during his explorations. However, he learned to navigate these experiences with resilience and courage, ultimately emerging with a deeper understanding of himself and the spiritual world.

Alan's spiritual journey is a profound testament to the transformative power of embracing the unknown and allowing oneself to be guided by the unseen forces of the universe. From his early life as an engineer rooted firmly in the material world to his eventual awakening to the spiritual realms, Alan's story is a beacon of hope and encouragement for others navigating similar paths.

While Alan's awakening began subtly, the more he would allow and accept the new experiences that challenged his understanding of reality, the more reality began to dissolve and form at once. These experiences were not always easy to comprehend, but they laid the foundation for a broader perspective on life and existence. The journey was marked by synchronicities, intuitive insights, and encounters with spiritual guides who helped him navigate the complexities of his spiritual path.

Throughout his journey, Alan learned several key lessons that can inspire and guide others:

1. Trust the Process: Alan's story underscores the importance of trusting the journey, even when it leads into the unknown. His experiences taught him that the universe often has plans beyond our immediate understanding, and trusting in this process can lead to profound growth and

transformation.

2. Embrace Synchronicities: Alan's life was filled with meaningful coincidences that guided him towards his spiritual awakening. These synchronicities, from meeting key individuals to experiencing pivotal events, served as reminders that there is a greater plan at work.

3. Spiritual Rebirth: One of the most transformative aspects of Alan's journey was his experience of spiritual rebirth. This rebirth was facilitated by various spiritual practices and guides, helping him shed old layers of his identity and embrace a new, more authentic self.

4. The Role of Guides: Alan's journey was supported by numerous spiritual guides, both seen and unseen. These guides provided him with the wisdom, support, and encouragement needed to navigate his path. His story highlights the importance of being open to receiving help from spiritual mentors and guides. These guides continued to support him during the conclusion of this book and at the end of his life.

5. Facing Challenges: Like any profound journey, Alan's path was not without its challenges. He faced moments of doubt, fear, and uncertainty. However, these challenges were integral to his

growth, teaching him resilience and the importance of perseverance.

Alan's journey is a source of inspiration for those embarking on their own spiritual paths. His experiences show that spiritual awakening is a deeply personal and transformative process that can lead to a greater understanding of oneself and the universe. By sharing his story, Alan hopes to offer comfort and guidance to others, helping them navigate their spiritual awakenings with courage and trust.

As Alan reflected on his journey, he leaves us with a powerful message: spiritual awakening is an ongoing process of growth and learning. It is a journey that requires openness, trust, and a willingness to embrace the unknown. Through his story, Alan invites us all to explore the depths of our own spiritual potential and to find meaning in the interconnectedness of all life.

Dream Journal Thoughts

Prison ... Prisoner ... Chains ... captive ...
Bound up ... straight jacket ... mad ...
crying ...

I.

Silence, bliss, peace, calm ....

A void ... nothing ... Oh ... but it can be wonderful.

To scream and shout ... to really let out the rage
and .... then to collapse in exhaustion ...

Observation, dreams, visions ...
what does any of this have to do with my class?
I don't know.
There! I did just observe ...
well maybe not like any one would expect, but it is my observation.

I am me. I am unique.

LOVE

There I said it. It was stuck in my mind for a while before it got to this page.

Love of life... Love of self... Love of all that is!
unconditional and complete love.

Thoughts from Alan's Dream Journal
Alan Jones

A Note from Alan

"As I look back at my life from the perspective of my late years I realize it has been a good life even with all of the challenges like losing all of our home equity, quitting my job and trying to build a small business that could support us.

If I had to do my life all over I would not change it.

I have many fond memories of growing up, going to college, raising a family and eventually spending the later years in small towns until Coralie was gone. After she was gone the only thing that saddens me other than her difficult final years is my dependence on others due to my own health issues.

Coralie and I lived at the end of a more idyllic era and were able to travel and see places that we enjoyed before they became over-developed and over-populated. Sometimes when I am watching movies I am drawn back to those earlier times. Coralie had many life challenges and I enjoyed helping her through those years even though she often frustrated me because I knew she had much more potential than she would admit.

I have also been blessed to have been shown how to change my life perspective through many life-altering experiences both physical and spiritual. Those experiences have been amazing and have revealed a reality that I would have never believed to exist had it not been for the intervention of those wonderful beings who came to my rescue when I had lost my life compass.

I recently wrote a letter to God expressing my frustrations with my current life but I ended that letter with this: God, I give special thanks for the help and guidance you have sent me in this lifetime and especially for the support provided by the spirits Ellen, Andrea and Ellen's mother that came to my rescue as well as the physical helpers Patricia Padilla, Mary Margaret, Coralie and all the others that have been there when I needed them. If I were to list all of those people that I want to thank I believe it would be absolutely every person I have known or met in this lifetime.

I missed thanking all of my unseen and unknown helpers and I do thank them as well. As I write these last thoughts I must give a very special thanks to Brianna Lafferty for making it possible for me to share my experiences and story.

I also thank my children and their families for their support and caring in my late years.

A special note about Patricia Padilla. Patricia was the hispanic curandera who enabled me to have the rebirth experience. She enabled the energy to flow with the use of acupuncture so that I could experience Ellen and Andrea. She also provided the support for me to experience two of my past lives.

To Randy and Dan,

I have really enjoyed being part of your life. I want to thank you again for helping me discard a lifetime collection of stuff and enabling my move to Denver.

To Kim,

Thank you for your support in all ways.You found a house where we could all live. You found the link that eventually enabled me to connect with Brianna and make this telling of my story possible.

Maybe the path to freedom is not through a single story but rather a collection of stories. A collection which is growing as more and more people come forward to share their experiences.

It is through us that reality is being created. What it becomes is up to us."

- Alan Jones

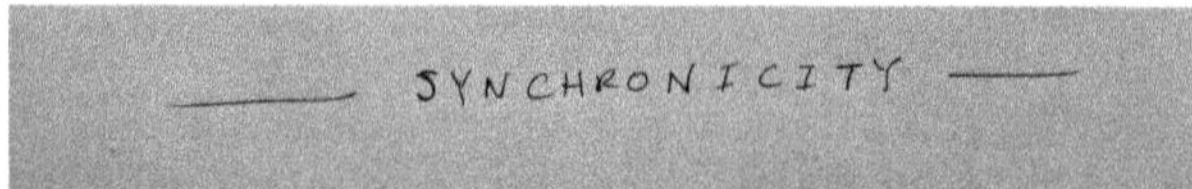

A theme Alan captured in his dream journal
Alan Jones

By the Sea - Poem

My Dream --- By The Sea

As I awaken I am soaring
Soaring high above green fields
Nearby is a sea
A sea that I can not see
You see

As I soar high above those green fields
I soar to the edge of the bluff
Near the sea
A sea that I can not see
You see

As I soar to the edge of the bluff
I soar down a fissure
To the sea
A sea that I can not see
You see

I soar below the bluff
Seeking the rising air
To lift me again high into the sky
To my left is the sea
A sea that I can not see
You see

I soar along the bluff

A sandy bluff
With its hues of pale yellow and tan
By the sea
A sea that I can not see
You see

As I watch the bluff
Umfff...
I bump into a whale
Soaring by the sea
A sea that I can not see
You see

A great giant whale
With his great white under belly
And giant tail above
As we soar by the sea
A sea that I can not see
You see

His belly, this belly of the whale
Is so soft, so smooth, so warm
I must keep my distance
As we soar by the sea
A sea that I can not see
You see

As I watch this great gray and white whale
I soon realize we are followed
By other creatures of the sea
A sea by the bluff
A sea that I can not see
You see

As we all soar in our single file
I am wondering
Are we in the sea
A sea that I have not dreamed
A sea that I can not see
You see

- Alan Jones

A Note from the Author

As I was asked to write Alan's story, I was struck by the synchronicities that brought us together. From the moment he saw me speak at the NDE group in Denver, to watching me on a podcast, reading my book "White Flame," and eventually becoming my client in the realm of Death and Spiritual Doulaing, our paths were intertwined by a higher purpose. Alan couldn't sleep the night after we met, guided by spirit to ask me to write his story. Similarly, I felt butterflies when spirit told me I needed to write his story. By telling Alan's story, he marks a significant milestone off his soul contract before departing this realm. As a Death Doula, capturing his legacy, and as a Spiritual Doula, understanding the soul's need to complete its contract, I am honored to share his journey with the world. Through his story, we hope to inspire, offer hope, and encourage transformation in others.

I am beyond honored and grateful to be asked to write the story of Alan Jones and his awakening process. This book came into existence through a harmonious blend of electronic and print files, virtual and in-person meetings, and, most importantly, the guiding hand of Destiny.

www.ingramcontent.com/pod-product-compliance
Ingram Content Group UK Ltd.
Pitfield, Milton Keynes, MK11 3LW, UK
UKHW021835270726
14058UKWH00002B/170

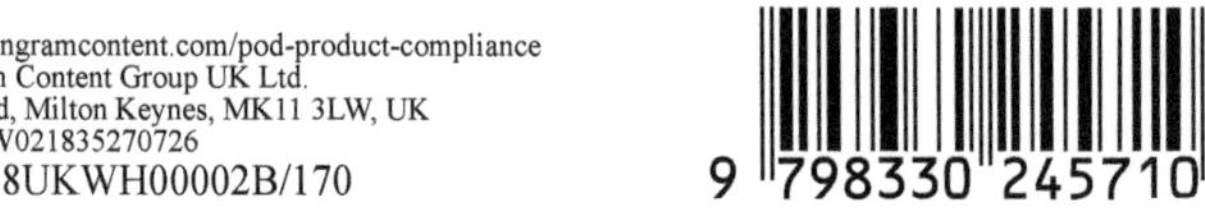